KAZAKHSTAN 2016 HUMAN RIGHTS REPORT

EXECUTIVE SUMMARY

The Republic of Kazakhstan has a government system dominated by President Nursultan Nazarbayev and the ruling Nur Otan Party. The constitution concentrates power in the presidency. The president controls the legislature and judiciary as well as regional and local governments. Changes or amendments to the constitution require presidential consent. The April 2015 presidential election, in which President Nazarbayev received 97.5 percent of the vote, was marked by irregularities and lacked genuine political competition. President Nazarbayev's Nur Otan Party won 82 percent of the vote in the March 2016, election for the Mazhilis (lower house of parliament). The Organization for Security and Cooperation in Europe (OSCE)/Office for Democratic Institutions and Human Rights (ODIHR) observation mission noted some progress but judged the country continued to require considerable progress to meet its OSCE commitments for democratic elections.

Civilian authorities maintained effective control over the security forces.

The most significant human rights problems were limits on citizens' ability to choose their government in free and fair elections; selective restrictions on freedoms of expression, press, assembly, religion, and association; and lack of an independent judiciary and due process, especially in dealing with pervasive corruption and abuses by law enforcement and judicial officials. The criminal and administrative codes that went into effect in 2015, as well as the trade union law, further limited freedoms of speech, assembly, and religion. Provisions of the criminal code prohibiting incitement of ethnic, religious, social, and other "discord" were particularly open to abuse.

Other reported abuses included arbitrary or unlawful killings; military hazing that led to deaths; detainee and prisoner torture and other abuse; harsh and sometimes life-threatening prison conditions; arbitrary arrest and detention; infringements on citizens' privacy rights; prohibitive political party registration requirements; restrictions on the activities of nongovernmental organizations (NGOs); violence and discrimination against women; abuse of children; sex and labor trafficking; discrimination against persons with disabilities; societal discrimination against lesbian, gay, bisexual, transgender, and intersex (LGBTI) persons; discrimination against those with HIV/AIDS; and child labor.

The government selectively prosecuted officials who committed abuses, especially in high-profile corruption cases; nevertheless, corruption remained widespread, and impunity existed for those in positions of authority as well as for those connected to government or law enforcement officials.

Section 1. Respect for the Integrity of the Person, Including Freedom from:

a. Arbitrary Deprivation of Life and other Unlawful or Politically Motivated Killings

There were reports the government or its agents committed arbitrary or unlawful killings or beatings that led to deaths.

On July 14, Erik Turekulov of Zhambyl region died after he was allegedly beaten by local police, who detained him for swimming in a no-swimming area near the Karakystak hydropower station. According to the doctors, Turekulov was brought to the hospital already in a coma, from which he failed to recover. The Zhambyl regional police department indicated it was looking into the actions of the police members who detained Turekulov. On December 14, a Zhambyl regional court convicted a police officer for abuse of power and infliction of grave injuries that led to negligent death. He was sentenced to nine years in prison. Two other police officers also involved in the beating remained under investigation.

Military hazing led to deaths, suicides, and serious injuries. On September 28, Private Urazgaliyev of Army Unit 32363 in Kapshagay died in the local hospital after a disagreement with the detachment commander, Sergeant Ramadin, who allegedly hit the conscript in the head. Urazgaliyev lost consciousness and was taken to the hospital, where he later died. Military prosecutors began an investigation of the incident, and Sergeant Ramadin was arrested. Due to the sensitivity of such cases, the Ministry of Defense rarely discloses additional information to the general public.

b. Disappearance

There were no reports of politically motivated disappearances.

c. Torture and Other Cruel, Inhuman, or Degrading Treatment or Punishment

The law prohibits torture; nevertheless, police and prison officials allegedly tortured and abused detainees. Human rights activists asserted the domestic legal definition of torture was noncompliant with the definition of torture in the UN Convention against Torture.

The National Preventive Mechanism (NPM) against Torture came into force in 2014 when the prime minister signed rules permitting the monitoring of institutions. Some observers commented that NPM staff lacked sufficient knowledge and training to recognize instances of torture. The NPM is part of the Office of the Human Rights Ombudsman and thus is not independent of the government. The human rights ombudsman reported during the year receiving 96 complaints alleging torture, violence, and other cruel and degrading treatment and punishment. In its March report covering activities in 2015, the NPM reported that the risk of human rights violations was high at temporary detention centers, especially in the first few hours. The Public Monitoring Commission (PMC) corroborated that report and elaborated that torture typically occurred during the initial period of detention. Suspects often were beaten during transit or in police stations.

The NGO Kazakhstan International Bureau for Human Rights and Rule of Law (KIBHR) recorded 115 complaints of torture in the first six months of the year. The prosecutor general indicated its office registered 600 torture complaints on average per year. Not all cases led to prosecution or conviction. The NGO Penal Reform International (PRI) indicated four of the 350 officially registered criminal investigations of torture went to court trial during the first 10 months of the year.

In June an inmate of prison LA-155/18 in the Almaty region, Natalya Slekishina, submitted a complaint to the Almaty police department that she had been raped by several prison officers. She subsequently gave birth to a child on April 25. DNA tests conducted by the Center of Forensic Examination under the Justice Ministry indicated a DNA match for Ruslan Hakimov, one of the four prison officers mentioned in Slekishina's complaint, as the child's biological father. Slekishina's lawyer, Aiman Umarova, a well-known human rights attorney, insisted the three other officers should be charged with rape as well. Umarova argued that other officers who were aware of the crime should also be held liable and that charges for torture should be added to the case, since they failed to stop the rape. Slekishina, who faced pressure and threats while under continued incarceration, chose not to press charges in the case further. On September 30, Hakimov was sentenced to nine years in prison.

Prison and Detention Center Conditions

Prison conditions were generally harsh and sometimes life threatening, and facilities did not meet international health standards. Health problems among prisoners went untreated in many cases, or prison conditions exacerbated them.

<u>Physical Conditions</u>: According to PRI, although men and women were held separately and pretrial detainees were held separately from convicted prisoners, during transitions between temporary detention centers, pretrial detention, and prisons, youths often were held with adults of the same sex.

Abuse occurred in police cells, pretrial detention facilities, and prisons. Observers cited the primary cause of mistreatment as the lack of professional training programs for administrators.

The NPM reported infrastructure problems in prisons, such as unsatisfactory sanitary and hygiene conditions, including poor plumbing and sewerage systems and unsanitary bedding. It also reported shortages of medical staff and insufficient medicine, as well as problems of mobility for prisoners with disabilities. In many places NPM noted restricted connectivity with the outside world and limited access to information about prisoners' rights. PRI reported there was a widespread lack of heating and adequate ventilation in prisons, noting that in some cases extreme temperatures threatened the health of the inmates.

The government did not publish statistics on the number of suicides or attempted suicides in pretrial detention centers or prisons during the year.

According to the Prosecutor General's Office, 54 cases of civil disobedience by prisoners were registered in 2016.

<u>Administration</u>: The law does not allow unapproved religious services, rites, ceremonies, meetings, or missionary activity in prisons. By law a prisoner in need of "religious rituals" or his relatives may ask to invite a representative of a registered religious organization to carry out religious rites, ceremonies, and/or meetings, provided they do not obstruct prison activity or violate the rights and legal interests of other individuals.

<u>Independent Monitoring</u>: There were no independent international monitors of prisons. The local independent monitoring group PMC visited approximately 340340 facilities during the first six months of the year.

Improvements: The 2015 criminal code introduced alternative sentences, including fines and public service, but human rights activists noted they were not implemented effectively.

d. Arbitrary Arrest or Detention

The law prohibits arbitrary arrest and detention, but the practice occurred. The government did not provide statistics on the number of individuals unlawfully detained during the year; prosecutors released 205 individuals who were unlawfully held in police cells and offices. KIBHR reported 106 incidents of unlawful detention of civil society activists. Authorities released on bail 2,000 suspects who were held in temporary custody while they awaited arrest authorization by the court.

Role of the Police and Security Apparatus

The Ministry of Internal Affairs supervises the national police force, which has primary responsibility for internal security, including investigation and prevention of crimes and administrative offenses, and maintenance of public order and security. The Agency of Civil Service Affairs and Anticorruption has administrative and criminal investigative powers. The Committee for National Security (KNB) plays a role in border security, internal and national security, antiterrorism efforts, and the investigation and interdiction of illegal or unregistered groups, such as extremist groups, military groups, political parties, religious groups, and trade unions. The KNB, Syrbar (the foreign intelligence service), and the Agency of Civil Service Affairs and Anticorruption all report directly to the president. Many government ministers maintained personal blogs where citizens could register complaints.

Although the government took some steps to prosecute officials who committed abuses, impunity existed, especially where corruption was involved or personal relationships with government officials were established.

Arrest Procedures and Treatment of Detainees

A person apprehended as a suspect in a crime is taken to a police office for interrogation. Prior to interrogation, the accused should have the opportunity to meet with an attorney. Upon arrest the investigator may do an immediate body search if there is a reason to believe the detainee has a gun or may try to discard or destroy evidence. Within three hours of arrest, the investigator is required to write a statement declaring the reason for the arrest, the place and time of the arrest, the results of the body search, and the time of writing the statement. It is then signed by the investigator and the detained suspect. The investigator should also submit a written report to the prosecutor's office within 12 hours of the signature of the statement.

The arrest must be approved by the court. It is a three-step procedure: (1) the investigator collects all evidence to justify the arrest and takes all materials of the case to the prosecutor; (2) the prosecutor studies the evidence and takes it to court within 12 hours; and (3) the court proceeding is held with the participation of the criminal suspect, his/her lawyer, and the prosecutor. If within 72 hours of the arrest the administration of the detention facility has not received a court decision approving the arrest, the administration should immediately release him/her and notify the officer who handles the case and the prosecutor. The court may choose other forms of restraint: house arrest, restriction of movement, or a written requirement not to leave the city/place of residence.

According to human rights activists, these procedures were frequently ignored.

Authorized bail procedures exist but were not used in many cases. Instead, prolonged pretrial detentions were commonplace.

Detainees may be held in pretrial detention for up to two months. The term may be extended up to 18 months if the investigation continues. Upon the completion of the investigation, the investigator puts together an official indictment. The materials of the case are shared with the defendant and then sent to the prosecutor, who has five days to check the materials and forward them to the court.

Although the judiciary has the authority to deny or grant arrest warrants, judges authorized prosecutor warrant requests in the vast majority of cases. Prosecutors continued to have the power to authorize investigative actions, such as search and seizure.

Persons detained, arrested, or accused of committing a crime have the right to the assistance of a defense lawyer from the moment of detention, arrest, or accusation. The 2015 criminal procedure code introduced an obligation for police to inform detainees about their rights, including the right to an attorney. Human rights observers alleged that prisoners were constrained in their ability to communicate with their attorneys and that penitentiary staff often remained present during the meetings between defendants and attorneys. During a July 15 public hearing in Astana, the well-known defense attorney Aiman Umarova reported that, in several cases, audio and video recording equipment was present in lawyer-client meeting rooms and case documents were often reviewed, disrupting the right to attorney-client confidentiality.

The human rights ombudsman reported that law enforcement officials dissuaded detainees from seeing an attorney, gathered evidence through preliminary questioning before a detainee's attorney arrived, and in some cases used defense attorneys to gather evidence. The law states that the government must provide an attorney for an indigent suspect or defendant when the suspect is a minor, has physical or mental disabilities, or faces serious criminal charges, but public defenders often lacked the necessary experience and training to assist defendants. Defendants are barred from freely choosing their defense counsel if the cases against them involve state secrets. The law allows only lawyers who have special clearance to work on such cases.

Arbitrary Arrest: Prosecutors reported continuing problems with arbitrary arrest and detention.

The government frequently arrested and detained political opponents and critics, sometimes for minor infractions, such as unsanctioned assembly, that led to fines or up to 10 days' administrative arrest. By law detainees may remain in pretrial detention for up to two months. Depending on the complexity and severity of the alleged offense, authorities may extend the term for up to 18 months while the investigation takes place. The pretrial detention term may not be longer than the potential sentence for the offense.

Pretrial Detention: The law allows police to hold a detainee for 72 hours before bringing charges. Human rights observers criticized this period as too lengthy and alleged that authorities often used this phase of detention to torture, beat, and abuse inmates to extract confessions.

The 2015 criminal code introduced the concept of conditional release on bail. The bail system is designed for persons who commit a criminal offense for the first time or for a crime of minor or moderate severity not associated with causing death or grievous bodily harm to the victim, provided that the penalties for committing such a crime contain a fine as an alternative penalty.

The law grants prisoners prompt access to family members, although authorities occasionally sent prisoners to facilities located far from their homes and relatives, thus preventing access for those unable to travel.

<u>Detainee's Ability to Challenge Lawfulness of Detention before a Court</u>: The Code of Criminal Procedure spells out a detainee's right to submit a complaint, challenge the justification for detention, or to seek a pre-trial probation as an alternative to arrest. Detainees have 15 days to submit complaints to the administration of the pre-trial detention facility or to local court. An investigative judge has three to 10 days to overturn or uphold the challenged decision.

e. Denial of Fair Public Trial

The law does not provide for an independent judiciary. The executive branch sharply limited judicial independence. Prosecutors enjoyed a quasi-judicial role and had the authority to suspend court decisions.

Corruption was evident at every stage of the judicial process. Although judges were among the most highly paid government employees, lawyers and human rights monitors alleged that judges, prosecutors, and other officials solicited bribes in exchange for favorable rulings in many criminal and civil cases.

Corruption in the judicial system was widespread. Bribes and irregular payments were regularly exchanged in order to obtain favorable court decisions. In many cases the courts were controlled by the interests of the ruling elite, according to Freedom House's Nations in Transition report for the year. Accordingly, public trust in the impartiality of the judicial system was low, and citizens held little expectation that justice would be dispensed professionally in court proceedings, as noted in the 2014 *Nations in Transition* Freedom House report. Recruitment of judges was plagued by corruption, and becoming a judge often required bribing various officials, according to the Bertelsmann Stiftung's Transformation Index report for the year.

Business entities were reluctant to approach courts as foreign businesses have a historically poor record when challenging government regulations and contractual disputes within the local judicial system. Judicial outcomes were perceived as subject to political influence and interference due to a lack of independence. Companies have also expressed reluctance to seek foreign arbitration as anecdotal evidence suggested the government looks unfavorably on cases involving foreign judicial entities.

According to Supreme Court Chairman Kairat Mami, one judge was convicted for corruption during the year. President Nazarbayev indicated at a national conference of judges that two judges were fired and 32 judges were disciplined during the first 10 months of the year.

Military courts have jurisdiction over civilian criminal defendants in cases allegedly connected to military personnel. Military courts use the same criminal code as civilian courts.

Trial Procedures

All defendants enjoy a presumption of innocence and are protected from self-incrimination under the law. Trials are public except in instances that could compromise state secrets or when necessary to protect the private life or personal family concerns of a citizen. At the beginning of the year, the list of crimes that may be handled through jury trials was expanded to include five more categories of particularly grave crimes.

Observers noted that the juror selection process was inconsistent. For example, on some occasions, the court learned after a trial concluded that a juror had a previous criminal conviction, which normally excludes potential members from the juror pool.

Indigent defendants in criminal cases have the right to counsel and a government-provided attorney. By law a defendant must be represented by an attorney when the defendant is a minor, has mental or physical disabilities, does not speak the language of the court, or faces 10 or more years of imprisonment. Defense attorneys, however, reportedly participated in only one-half of criminal cases, in part because the government failed to pay them properly or on time. The law also provides defendants the rights to be present at their trials, to be heard in court, to confront witnesses against them, and to call witnesses for the defense. They have the right to appeal a decision to a higher court. According to observers, prosecutors dominated trials, and defense attorneys played a minor role.

Domestic and international human rights organizations reported numerous problems in the judicial system, including lack of access to court proceedings, lack of access to government-held evidence, frequent procedural violations, denial of defense counsel motions, and failure of judges to investigate allegations that authorities extracted confessions through torture or duress.

Lack of due process was a problem, particularly in a handful of politically motivated trials involving protests by opposition activists and in cases in which there were allegations of improper political or financial influence.

Human rights and international observers noted investigative and prosecutorial practices that emphasized a confession of guilt over collection of other evidence in building a criminal case against a defendant. Courts generally ignored allegations by defendants that officials obtained confessions by torture or duress.

Political Prisoners and Detainees

A group of civil society activists maintained a list of individuals they considered detained or imprisoned based on politically motivated charges.

Land code activists Maks Bokayev and Talgat Ayan were convicted and sentenced to five years in prison on November 28 after a six-week trial on criminal code charges of incitement of social discord (Article 174), intentional dissemination of false information (Article 274), and holding an unsanctioned rally (Article 400). At no point during the peaceful protests did Bokayev or Ayan go beyond advocacy or dissent to commit acts of violence. Human rights observers, in the country and internationally, criticized the charges as a threat to the freedoms of speech, peaceful assembly, and political expression. Amnesty International termed the activists "prisoners of conscience." Specifically, Maina Kiai, UN special rapporteur for the Office of the High Commissioner for Human Rights, emphasized that under international law authorities could not impose authorization requirements on those seeking to hold peaceful assemblies and highlighted the danger of unclear or vague laws being interpreted in ways that could criminalize peaceful dissent.

On August 19, opposition figure Vladimir Kozlov was released on parole from prison, where he had served four and one-half years of his prison sentence of seven and one-half years. Kozlov had been convicted for creating and leading an extremist group, inciting social discord, and calling for the violent overthrow of the government. Observers believed these were politically motivated charges related to Kozlov's role as leader of the opposition party Alga.

Civil Judicial Procedures and Remedies

Individuals and organizations may seek civil remedies for human rights violations through domestic courts. Economic and administrative court judges handle civil cases under a court structure that largely mirrors the criminal court structure. Although the law and constitution provide for judicial resolution of civil disputes, observers viewed civil courts as corrupt and unreliable.

f. Arbitrary or Unlawful Interference with Privacy, Family, Home, or Correspondence

The constitution and law prohibit violations of privacy, but the government at times infringed on these rights.

The law provides prosecutors with extensive authority to limit citizens' constitutional rights. The KNB, the Ministry of Internal Affairs, and other agencies, with the concurrence of the Prosecutor General's Office, may infringe on the secrecy of private communications and financial records, as well as on the inviolability of the home. Lawyers and family members indicated the private documents and court evidence for Maks Bokayev were confiscated by police while he was meeting with his lawyer during pre-trial detention.

Courts may hear an appeal of a prosecutor's decision but may not issue an immediate injunction to cease an infringement. The law allows wiretapping in medium, urgent, and grave cases.

Government opponents, human rights defenders, and their family members continued to report the government occasionally monitored their movements.

In July human rights defender Amangeldy Shormanbayev of the NGO International Legal Initiative (ILI) posted a message on Facebook saying, "Our office is under open surveillance." In early August the State Revenue Agency began tax inspections of the NGO, and the group's leaders believed the actions were related to their plans to challenge new amendments to NGO laws.

Section 2. Respect for Civil Liberties, Including:

a. Freedom of Speech and Press

While the constitution provides for freedom of speech and of the press, the government limited freedom of expression and exerted influence on media through a variety of means, including laws, harassment, licensing regulations, internet restrictions, and criminal and administrative charges. Judicial actions against journalists and media outlets, including civil and criminal libel suits filed by government officials, led to the suspension of several media outlets and encouraged self-censorship. The law provides for additional measures and restrictions during "social emergencies," defined as "an emergency on a certain territory caused by contradictions and conflicts in social relations that may cause or have caused loss of life, personal injury, significant property damage, or violation of conditions of the population." In these situations the government may censor media sources by requiring them to provide their print, audio, and video information to authorities 24 hours before issuance/broadcasting for approval. Political parties and public associations may be suspended or closed should they obstruct the efforts of security forces. Regulations also allow the government to restrict or ban copying equipment, broadcasting equipment, and audio and video recording devices and temporarily seize sound-enhancing equipment.

Freedom of Speech and Expression: The government limited individual ability to criticize the country's leadership, and regional leaders attempted to limit criticism of their actions in local media. The law prohibits insulting the president or the president's family.

The 2015 criminal code penalizes "intentionally spreading false information" with fines of up to 12.96 million tenge ($40,000) and imprisonment for up to 10 years. For example, Kazkommertsbank, one of the largest banks in the country, sued the web portal *nakanune.kz* for publishing a reader's letter. The bank claimed the website published false information implicating the bank in corruption. On May 23, Baydalinova was sentenced to 18 months' incarceration. On July 12, the court suspended her sentence.

The criminal code penalizes "inciting social, national, tribal, racial, or religious discord" with imprisonment of up to 20 years. Civil society activist Zhanat Yesentayev was arrested in Uralsk on May 17, amid land reform protests. He was charged with incitement of interethnic discord in social media. In July he agreed to a plea bargain and was sentenced to two years and six months of restriction of freedom and a ban on participation in public protests, public performances, and posting any messages in social media on public, political, social, or environmental issues.

On January 21, a court in Astana sentenced civil society activist Bolatbek Blyalov to three years of restriction of freedom, meaning he was restricted to his city of residence and required legal supervision in the manner of parole, for instigation of ethnic and social discord. Blyalov had posted videos against the use of heptyl fuel, a highly toxic Russian Proton rocket fuel, at Baikonur cosmodrome.

On January 23, a court in Almaty convicted Serikzhan Mambetalin and Yermek Narymbayev, finding that their October 2015 social media postings incited social discord and insulted the honor and dignity of the country. The court sentenced Narymbayev to three years in jail and Mambetalin to two years in jail. On January 29, Mambetalin was released from prison after he publicly repented his actions. His prison term was replaced with a one-year restriction of freedom and a three-year ban on public activity. On March 30, a court replaced Narymbayev's prison term with three years' restriction of freedom and prohibited him from participating in public activities for five years. On July 14, he reportedly fled the country.

Press and Media Freedoms: Many privately owned newspapers and television stations received government subsidies. The lack of transparency in media ownership and the dependence of many outlets on government contracts for media coverage are significant problems. Companies allegedly controlled by members of the president's family or associates owned many of the broadcast media outlets that the government did not control outright. According to media observers, the government wholly or partly owned most of the nationwide television broadcasters. Regional governments owned several frequencies, and the Ministry of Investment and Development distributed those frequencies to independent broadcasters via a tender system.

All media are required to register with the Ministry of Information and Communication, although websites are exempt from this requirement. The law limits the simultaneous broadcast of foreign-produced programming to 20 percent of a locally based station's weekly broadcast time. This provision burdened smaller, less-developed regional television stations that lacked resources to create programs, although the government did not sanction any media outlet under this provision. Foreign media broadcasting does not have to meet this requirement.

Violence and Harassment: According to the NGO Adil Soz, through August authorities prevented reporters from carrying out their duties in 86 instances; 57 of them occurred during the May 21 land protests. Adil Soz found that authorities denied or significantly restricted journalists' access to public information 114 times.

Journalists working in opposition media and covering stories related to corruption reported harassment and intimidation by government officials and private actors.

The president of the Kazakhstan Union of Journalists and former spokesman for President Nazarbayev, Seitkazy Matayev, was arrested in Almaty on February 22 on charges of tax evasion and embezzlement of state funds related to his news agency KazTAG's government contracts. (Like many other media outlets in the country, KazTAG maintained contracts with the government for media coverage.) On October 3, a judge in Astana sentenced Matayev to six years in prison and his son, Aset, the director of the news agency, to five years and confiscation of business-related real estate property and assets.

On April 19, Tamara Kaleyeva from the NGO Adil Soz was elected to replace Matayev as the new head of the Union of Journalists. Since her appointment, however, she and the organization have been subjected to three on-site tax audits.

<u>Censorship or Content Restrictions</u>: The law enables the government to restrict media content through amendments that prohibit undermining state security or advocating class, social, race, national, or religious discord. Owners, editors, distributors, and journalists may be held civilly and criminally responsible for content unless it came from an official source. The government used this provision to restrict media freedom.

The law allows the prosecutor general to suspend access to the internet and other means of communication without a court order. In cases where communication networks were used "for criminal purposes to harm the interests of an individual, society, or the state, or to disseminate information violating the Election Law… or containing calls for extremist or terrorist activities, riots, or participation in large-scale (public) activities carried out in violation of the established order," the prosecutor general may suspend communication services.

By law internet resources, including social media, are classified as forms of mass media and governed by the same rules and regulations. Several bloggers and social media users were charged with inciting social discord through their posts and sentenced to imprisonment. Civic activists and bloggers Serikzhan Mambetalin and Yermek Narymbayev were sentenced to two and three years in jail respectively on January 22 on charges of "inciting interethnic hatred discord" by posting excerpts of an unpublished book about Kazakhstan's dependence on Russia. Their sentences were later reduced to house arrest.

Pavlodar resident Ruslan Ginatullin was detained July 5 after posting social media page links to two YouTube videos, one discussing "Russian Nazis" and the other on the conflict in Ukraine. Ministry of Justice "experts" determined content in the two videos incited interethnic discord. Ginatullin's lawyer said the charges were baseless, and his client was a staunch pacifist who posted the videos to warn individuals against war and extremism. A blogger in Aktobe, Sanat Dosov, went on trial November 29, also charged with inciting social discord for allegedly posting articles critical of Russian President Putin.

Libel/Slander Laws: The law provides enhanced penalties for libel against senior government officials. Private parties may initiate criminal libel suits without independent action by the government, and an individual filing such a suit may also file a civil suit based on the same allegations. Officials used the law's libel and defamation provisions to restrict media outlets from publishing unflattering information. Both the criminal and civil codes contain articles establishing broad liability for libel, with no statute of limitation or maximum amount of compensation. The requirement that owners, editors, distributors, publishing houses, and journalists prove the veracity of published information, regardless of its source, encouraged self-censorship at each level.

The law includes penalties for defamatory remarks made in the mass media or "information-communication networks," including heavy fines and prison terms. Journalists and human rights activists feared these provisions would strengthen the government's ability to restrict investigative journalism.

NGOs reported that libel cases against journalists and media outlets remained a problem. Media freedom NGO Adil Soz reported 47 criminal libel charges, with four ending in conviction, and 55 civil libel lawsuits filed against journalists and media. Only 17 cases were ruled in favor of journalists. Adil Soz indicated the numbers represented a nearly fourfold increase in criminal cases against media outlets and individual journalists over the last two years. On July 12, an Almaty court ruled an article in the independent *Tribuna* newspaper harmed the dignity and honor of Sultanbek Syzdykov, the former director for organizing the Asian Winter Games "Asiada-2011," and imposed an administrative fine of five million tenge ($15,000) on the author of the publication and the newspaper. The newspaper filed an appeal that the courts rejected in October.

National Security: The law criminalizes the release of information regarding the health, finances, or private life of the president, as well as economic information, such as data about mineral reserves or government debts to foreign creditors. To avoid possible legal problems, media outlets often practiced self-censorship regarding the president and his family.

The law prohibits "influencing public and individual consciousness to the detriment of national security through deliberate distortion and spreading of unreliable information." Legal experts noted the term "unreliable information" is overly broad. The law also requires owners of communication networks and service providers to obey the orders of authorities in case of terrorist attacks or to suppress mass riots.

The law prohibits publication of any statement that promotes or glorifies "extremism" or "incites social discord," terms that international legal experts noted the government did not clearly define. The government subjected to intimidation media outlets that criticized the president; such intimidation included law enforcement actions and civil suits. Although these actions continued to have a chilling effect on media outlets, some criticism of government policies continued. Incidents of local government pressure on media continued.

Internet Freedom

Observers reported the government blocked or slowed access to opposition websites. Many observers believe the government added progovernment postings and opinions in internet chat rooms. The government regulated the country's internet providers, including majority state-owned Kazakhtelecom. Nevertheless, websites carried a wide variety of views, including viewpoints critical of the government. Official statistics reported more than 70 percent of the population had internet access in 2016.

The Ministry of Information and Communication controlled the registration of ".kz" internet domains. Authorities may suspend or revoke registration for locating servers outside the country. Observers criticized the registration process as unduly restrictive and vulnerable to abuse.

The government implemented regulations on internet access that mandated surveillance cameras in all internet cafes, required visitors to present identification to use the internet, demanded internet cafes keep a log of visited websites, and authorized law enforcement officials to access the names and internet histories of users. In 2014 the president signed a law further restricting freedoms of communication (see section 2.a.).

NGO Adil Soz reported that during the first nine months, courts blocked 55 websites for propaganda of religious extremism and terrorism.

In several cases the government denied it was behind the blocking of websites. Bloggers reported anecdotally their sites were periodically blocked, as did the publishers of independent news sites *ratel.kz*, *zonakz.net*, and *uralskweek.kz*, as well as the website of the banned newspaper *Respublika*. Radio Azattyk reported that some of its news reports were not accessible in the country. During the May 21 protest rallies, there were multiple reports that access to social media, including YouTube, was partially or fully blocked.

Government surveillance was also prevalent. According to the 2016 *Freedom on the Net* report, Facebook users who planned to take part in protests reported several times they received police visits to their residences to "discuss their Facebook posts" and warn them against going to an unsanctioned gathering. The report noted internet users reported difficulties in accessing social media and communication apps during the land reform protests. In January activists utilizing social media announced and coordinated an unauthorized peaceful rally in support of the *ADAMbol* magazine, but authorities detained key participants--including journalists and human rights activists--near their residences as they were heading to the gathering. Civil society activists who discussed on social media their plans to take part in the May 21 land protests reported police visits to their residences to warn them against going to an unsanctioned gathering. On December 9, the Almaty specialized administrative court convicted civil society activist Almat Zhumagulov for re-posting another activist's Facebook statement calling people to rally on the Independence Day and sentenced him to a 15-day administrative arrest.

Freedom on the Net reported during the year that the country maintained a system of operative investigative measures that allowed the government to use surveillance methods called Deep Packet Inspection (DPI). While Kazakhtelecom maintained that it used its DPI system for traffic management, there were reports that Check Point Software Technologies installed the system on its backbone infrastructure in 2010. The report added that a regulator adopted a new internet monitoring technology, the Automated System of Monitoring the National Information Space.

Academic Freedom and Cultural Events

The government generally did not restrict academic freedom, although general restrictions, such as the prohibition on infringing on the dignity and honor of the president and his family, also applied to academics. Many academics practiced self-censorship.

b. Freedom of Peaceful Assembly and Association

Freedom of Assembly

The law provides for limited freedom of assembly, but there were significant restrictions on this right, and police used force to disrupt peaceful demonstrations. The law defines unsanctioned gatherings, public meetings, demonstrations, marches, picketing, and strikes that upset social and political stability as national security threats.

The law includes penalties for organizing or participating in illegal gatherings and for providing organizational support in the form of property, means of communication, equipment, and transportation, if the enumerated actions cause significant damage to the rights and legal interests of citizens, entities, or legally protected interests of the society or the government.

By law organizations must apply to local authorities for a permit to hold a demonstration or public meeting at least 10 days in advance. Opposition figures and human rights monitors complained that complicated and vague procedures and the 10-day notification period made it difficult for groups to organize public meetings and demonstrations and noted local authorities turned down many applications for demonstrations or only allowed them to take place outside the city center.

Authorities often briefly detained and fined organizers of unsanctioned gatherings. The NGO KIBHR, which monitored demonstrations in nine cities, recorded 19 peaceful demonstrations during the year, none of which were sanctioned by the government.

In April and May, a series of unsanctioned peaceful protests took place in a number of cities. Participants protested a law extending the period during which agricultural land could be leased to foreigners. On April 24, the first rally was held in Atyrau, despite local authorities' denying permission, followed by more protests three days later in Aktobe and Semey. Government authorities for the most part did not use force against the protesters, trying instead to dissuade them from the gatherings.

Activists of the protest movement used social media to announce plans to hold nationwide protests May 21. While more than 1,700 activists and 50 reporters were detained in different cities on May 21, most were released the same day. According to official statistics, 51 individuals were brought to court, four were sentenced to administrative arrests, 13 were fined, and 34 were given warnings.

Law enforcement officials also detained a number of activists throughout the country in the lead-up to the May 21 protests.

Two activists in Atyrau, Max Bokayev and Talgat Ayan, were arrested May 17 and charged with organizing unsanctioned protests, inciting social discord, and intentionally spreading false information. Their court trial began on October 12, following repeated extensions of pretrial detention that amounted to nearly five months. During detention Bokayev reportedly suffered from health problems, but the court denied his release to house arrest, citing a risk of flight.

Authorities repeatedly denied applications by civil society activists to hold peaceful protest actions in support of Bokayev and Ayan, with the justification protest actions would exert pressure on the court proceedings. On October 23, a group of activists gathered in Almaty to demonstrate their support for the two. Police arrested five protesters, with three sentenced to 10-day administrative arrests. Other activists supporting Bokayev and Ayan reported harassment by authorities or being prevented from traveling to observe the trial.

Maina Kiai, UN special rapporteur on the rights to freedom of peaceful assembly and of association, provided a legal analysis of the Bokayev and Ayan case, expressing concern over the implications for freedom of assembly and highlighting the danger of vague laws being applied selectively in ways that criminalize peaceful dissent. KIBHR director and leading human rights activist Yevgeniy Zhovtis criticized the charges as a threat to freedoms of speech and peaceful assembly, as well as to political dialogue in the country.

On November 28, Bokayev and Ayan were sentenced to five years in prison, as well as fines and three years' deprivation of public activity. Supporters in the courtroom who chanted and sang to register their disagreement were urged to disperse as they had not been authorized in advance to protest.

Freedom of Association

The law provides for limited freedom of association, but there were significant restrictions on this right. Any public organization set up by citizens, including religious groups, must be registered with the Ministry of Justice, as well as with the local departments of justice in every region in which the organization conducts activities. The law requires public or religious associations to define their specific activities, and any association that acts outside the scope of its charter may be warned, fined, suspended, or ultimately banned. Participation in unregistered public organizations may result in administrative or criminal penalties, such as fines, imprisonment, the closure of an organization, or suspension of its activities.

NGOs reported some difficulty in registering public associations. According to government information, there were discrepancies in the submitted documents. The special rapporteur encouraged authorities to facilitate the formation of public associations proactively, since they could play a crucial role in advancing human rights and development.

Membership organizations other than religious groups, covered under separate legislation, must have at least 10 members to register at the local level and must have branches in more than half the country's regions for national registration. The government considered political parties and labor unions to be membership organizations but required political parties to have 40,000 signatures for registration. If authorities challenge the application by alleging irregular signatures, the registration process may continue only if the total number of eligible signatures exceeds the minimum number required. The law prohibits parties established on an ethnic, gender, or religious basis. The law also prohibits members of the armed forces, employees of law enforcement and other national security organizations, and judges from participating in trade unions or political parties.

According to Special Rapporteur Kiai, the law regulating the establishment of political parties is problematic as it imposes onerous obligations prior to registration, including high initial membership requirements that prevent small parties from forming and extensive documentation that requires time and significant expense to collect. He also expressed concern regarding the broad discretion granted to officials in charge of registering proposed parties, noting that the process lacked transparency and the law allows for perpetual extensions of time for the government to review a party's application.

In 2015 parliament passed amendments to NGO financing laws that include new provisions governing registration and recordkeeping. Under the new law, all "nongovernment organizations, subsidiaries, and representative offices of foreign and international noncommercial organizations" are required to provide information on "their activities, including information about the founders, assets, sources of their funds and what they are spent on…." An "authorized body" may initiate a "verification" of the information submitted based on information received in mass media reports, complaints from individuals and entities, or other subjective sources. Untimely or inaccurate information contained in the report, discovered during verification, is an administrative offense and may carry fines up to 53,025 tenge ($159) or suspension for three months in case the violation is not rectified or is repeated within one year. In extreme cases criminal penalties are possible, which may lead to a large fine, suspension, or closure of the organization.

The law prohibits illegal interference by members of public associations in the activities of the government, with a fine of up to 636,300 tenge ($1,910) or imprisonment for up to 75 days. If committed by the leader of the organization, the fine may be up to 1.06 million tenge ($3,180) or imprisonment for no more than 90 days. The law does not clearly define "illegal interference."

Under the law a public association, along with its leaders and members, may face fines for performing activities outside its charter. The delineation between actions an NGO member takes in his or her private capacity versus as part of an organization is not clear in the law.

An NGO observer estimated that 20 of the almost 27,000 formally registered NGOs in the country remain independent of the government. In February the NGO International Legal Initiative (ILI) filed a lawsuit against the Ministry of Sports and Culture, claiming that the rules for compilation of ILI's database did not comply with legislation. In On July 1, the Astana economic court, and on September 7 its appellate panel, both rejected the NGO's lawsuit.

At least one NGO, Caspi Tabigaty in Atyrau, ceased operations, citing the redundancy and burden of the new requirements.

On July 26, the president of the country signed legislation affecting civil society organizations. The law includes reporting requirements concerning the receipt and expenditure of foreign funds or assets, and a requirement to label all publications produced with support from foreign funds as such. The Law on Payments also introduces administrative and criminal penalties for noncompliance with these new requirements and potential restrictions on the conduct of meetings, protests, and similar activities organized with foreign funds.

c. Freedom of Religion

See the Department of State's *International Religious Freedom Report* at
www.state.gov/religiousfreedomreport/.

d. Freedom of Movement, Internally Displaced Persons, Protection of Refugees, and Stateless Persons

The law provides for freedom of internal movement, foreign travel, emigration, and repatriation. Despite some regulatory restrictions, the government generally respected these rights. The government cooperated with the Office of the UN High Commissioner for Refugees (UNHCR) and other humanitarian organizations to provide protection and assistance to internally displaced persons, refugees, returning refugees, asylum seekers, stateless persons, and other persons of concern.

Human rights activists noted numerous violations of labor migrants' rights, particularly those of unregulated migrants. Labor migrants from neighboring Central Asian countries are often low skilled and seek manual labor. They are exposed to dangerous work and often face abusive practices. The migrants find themselves in vulnerable positions because of their unregulated legal status; the laborers do not know their rights, national labor and migration legislation, local culture, or the language. Among major violations of these migrants' rights, activists mentioned the lack of employment contracts, poor working conditions, long working hours, low salaries, nonpayment or delayed payment of salaries, and lack of decent housing. Migrant workers face the risk of falling victim to human trafficking and forced labor, and the International Labor Organization indicated migrants had very limited or no access to the justice system, social support, or basic health services.

In-country Movement: The government required foreigners who remained in the country for more than five days to register with migration police. Foreigners entering the country had to register at certain border posts or airports where they entered. Some foreigners experienced problems traveling in regions outside their registration area. The government's *Concept on Improving Migration Policy* covers internal migration, repatriation of ethnic Kazakh returnees (oralmans), and external labor migration. In April the government amended the rules for migrants entering the country so that migrants from Eurasian Economic Union countries may stay up to 90 days. There is a registration exemption for families of legal migrant workers for a 30-day period after the worker starts employment. The government has broad authority to deport those who violate the regulations.

Since 2011 the government has not reported the number of foreigners deported for gross violation of visitor rules. Individuals facing deportation may request asylum if they fear persecution in their home country. The government required persons who were suspects in criminal investigations to sign statements they would not leave their city of residence.

Authorities required foreigners to obtain prior permission to travel to certain border areas adjoining China and cities in close proximity to military installations. The government continued to declare particular areas closed to foreigners due to their proximity to military bases and the space launch center at Baikonur.

Foreign Travel: The government did not require exit visas for temporary travel of citizens, yet there were certain instances in which the government may deny exit from the country, including in the case of travelers subject to pending criminal or civil proceedings or having unfulfilled prison sentences, unpaid taxes, fines, alimony or utility bills, or compulsory military duty. Travelers who present false documentation during the exit process may be denied the right to exit, and authorities controlled travel by active-duty military personnel. The law requires persons who had access to state secrets to obtain permission from their employing government agency for temporary exit from the country.

Exile: The law does not prohibit forced exile if authorized by an appropriate government agency or through a court ruling.

Emigration and Repatriation: The law provides for the right to emigrate and the right to repatriate, and the government generally respected these rights. An exception is the law on national security, which prohibits persons who had access to state secrets from taking up permanent residence abroad for five years after leaving government service. The government required a permanent exit visa for emigration. Obtaining this visa required criminal checks, credit checks, and letters from parents and any dependents older than age 10 expressing no objection to exit visa issuance.

Protection of Refugees

The government cooperated with UNHCR and other organizations to provide protection and assistance to refugees from countries where their lives or freedom would be threatened on account of their race, religion, nationality, membership in a particular social group, or political opinion. The government recognized 38 persons as refugees during the first six months of the year, out of 84 asylum seekers at various stages of the process.

Access to Asylum: The law provides for the granting of asylum or refugee status, and the government has established a system for providing protection to refugees. UNHCR legally may appeal to the government and intervene on behalf of individuals facing deportation. The law and several implementing regulations and bylaws regulate the granting of asylum and refugee status.

The Refugee Status Determination outlines procedures and access to government services, including the right to be legally registered and issued official documents. The Department of Migration Police in the Ministry of Internal Affairs conducts status determination procedures. Any individual seeking asylum in the country has access to the asylum procedure. According to UNHCR, the staff assigned for asylum processing lacked knowledge and qualifications, and decisions often contradicted existing national legislation and provisions of the 1951 convention or applicable international standards. UNHCR also noted that the application of refugee criteria was not consistent throughout the country, and the recognition rate remained low. Reports indicated that regional authorities also discouraged some asylum seekers from applying for asylum.

A legislative framework does not exist to manage the movement of asylum seekers between the country's borders and authorities in other areas. There are no reception facilities for asylum seekers. The government does not provide accommodation, allowances, or any social benefits to asylum seekers. The law does not provide for differentiated procedures for persons with specific needs, such as separated children and persons with disabilities. Asylum seekers and refugees with specific needs are not entitled to financial or medical assistance. There are no guidelines for handling sensitive cases, including LGBTI cases.

The law envisages refugees as individuals fleeing persecution because of their race, religion, nationality, membership in a particular social group, or political opinion. It does not envisage protection to be provided to persons fleeing wars or situation of generalized violence. Authorities appeared to use this scenario in the asylum applications of persons fleeing Syria and Ukraine.

In March Syrian citizen Iasser Aliziddin, who is married to a Kazakhstani woman and has five children with her, was denied refugee asylum status by a court in

Karaganda. Under existing legislation war is not listed as a reason for granting such status. In May he lost an appeal to maintain status, and he and their five children faced having to leave the country. At year's end he was working with UNHCR to stay in country and resolve his status.

Employment: Refugees face difficulties in gaining employment and social assistance from the government. By law refugees have the right to work, with the exception of engaging in individual entrepreneurship. Refugees faced difficulties in accessing the labor market due to local employers' lack of awareness of refugee rights.

Access to Basic Services: All refugees recognized by the government receive a refugee certificate that allows them to stay in the country legally. The majority of refugees have been residing in the country for many years. Their status as "temporarily residing aliens" hinders their access to the full range of rights stipulated in the 1951 convention and the law. Refugee status lasts for one year and is subject to annual renewal. In view of their temporary status, refugees do not have the right to apply for nationality, including after permanently residing in the country for more than five years. Children of refugees born in the country are also not recognized as citizens and would be stateless or at risk of statelessness if their nationality in the country of origin of their parents may not be conferred. The law also lacks provisions on treatment of asylum seekers and refugees with specific needs. Refugees have no access to social benefits or allowances.

UNHCR reported cordial relations with the government in assisting refugees and asylum seekers. The government usually allowed UNHCR access to detained foreigners to ensure proper treatment and fair determination of status.

The government was generally tolerant in its treatment of local refugee populations.

Consistent with the Minsk Convention on Migration within the Commonwealth of Independent States (CIS), the government did not recognize Chechens as refugees. Chechens are eligible for temporary legal resident status for up to 180 days, as are any other CIS citizens. This temporary registration is renewable, but local migration officials have discretion over the renewal process.

The government has an agreement with China not to tolerate the presence of ethnic separatists from one country on the territory of the other. UNHCR reported no new cases of Uighur refugees during the year.

Stateless Persons

The constitution and law provide avenues to deal with those considered stateless, and the government generally took seriously its obligation to ease the burden of statelessness within the country. As of June 30, there were 6,876 persons officially registered by the government as stateless. The majority of individuals residing in the country with undetermined nationality, with de facto statelessness, or at heightened risk of statelessness are primarily those who have no identity documents have invalid identity documents from a neighboring CIS country, or are holders of Soviet-era passports. These individuals typically resided in remote areas without obtaining official documentation.

According to UNHCR the law provides a range of rights to persons recognized by the government as stateless. The legal status of officially registered stateless persons is documented and considered as having permanent residency, which is granted for 10 years in the form of a stateless person certificate. According to the law, after five years of residence in the country, stateless persons are eligible to apply for citizenship. Children born in the country to officially recognized stateless persons who have a permanent place of residence are recognized as nationals. A legal procedure exists for ethnic Kazakhs; those with immediate relatives in the country; and citizens of Ukraine, Belarus, Russia, and Kyrgyzstan, with which the country has agreements. The law gives the government six months to consider an application for citizenship. Some applicants complained that, due to the lengthy bureaucratic process, obtaining citizenship often took years. In summary the law does not provide a simplified naturalization procedure for stateless persons. Existing legislation prevents children of parents without identity documents from obtaining birth certificates, which hindered their access to education, free health care, and freedom of movement.

Persons rejected or whose status of stateless persons has been revoked may appeal the decision, but such appeals involved a lengthy process.

Officially recognized stateless persons have access to free medical assistance on the level provided to other foreigners, but it is limited to emergency medical care and to treatment of 21 contagious diseases on a list approved by the Ministry of Healthcare and Social Development. Officially recognized stateless persons have a right to employment, with the exception of government positions. They may face challenges when concluding labor contracts, since potential employers may not understand or be aware of this legal right.

UNHCR reported that stateless persons without identity documents may not legally work, which led to the growth of illegal labor migration, corruption, and abuse of authority among employers. Children accompanying stateless parents were also considered stateless.

Section 3. Freedom to Participate in the Political Process

The constitution and law provide citizens the ability to choose their government in free and fair periodic elections held by secret ballot and based on universal and equal suffrage, but the government severely limited exercise of this right.

Although the 2007 constitutional amendments increased legislative authority in some spheres, the constitution continues to concentrate power in the presidency. The president appoints and dismisses most high-level government officials, including the prime minister, cabinet, prosecutor general, KNB chief, Supreme Court and lower-level judges, and regional governors. The Mazhilis must confirm the president's choice of prime minister, and the Senate must confirm the president's choices of prosecutor general, KNB chief, Supreme Court judges, and National Bank head. Parliament has never failed to confirm a presidential nomination. Modifying or amending the constitution effectively requires the president's consent. Constitutional amendments exempt President Nazarbayev from the two-term presidential term limit and protect him from prosecution.

Two laws, termed "Leader-of-the-Nation laws," establish President Nazarbayev as chair of the Kazakhstan People's Assembly, grant him lifetime membership on the Constitutional and Security Councils, allow him "to address the people of Kazakhstan at any time," and stipulate that all "initiatives on the country's development" must be coordinated through him.

Elections and Political Participation

Recent Elections: An early presidential election in April 2015 gave President Nazarbayev 97.5 percent of the vote. According to the *New York Times*, his two opponents, who supported the Nazarbayev government, were seen as playing a perfunctory role as opposition candidates. The Organization for Security and Cooperation in Europe (OSCE) stated that the election process generally was managed effectively, although the OSCE/Office for Democratic Institutions and Human Rights (ODIHR) election observation mission stated that voters were not given a choice of political alternatives and noted both "opposition" candidates had openly praised Nazarbayev's achievements and some voters reportedly had been pressured to vote for the incumbent.

As a result of early Mazhilis elections on March 20, the ruling Nur Otan Party won 84 seats, Ak Zhol won seven seats, and the Communist People's Party of Kazakhstan won seven seats. The official statistic for turnout was 77.2 percent, yet ODIHR reported widespread ballot stuffing and inflated vote totals. ODIHR criticized the election for falling short of the country's democratic commitments. The legal framework imposed substantial restrictions on fundamental civil and political rights. On election day serious procedural errors and irregularities were noted during voting, counting, and tabulation.

Political Parties and Political Participation: Political parties must register members' personal information, including date and place of birth, address, and place of employment. This requirement discouraged many citizens from joining political parties.

There were seven political parties registered, including Ak Zhol, Birlik, and the People's Patriotic Party "Auyl" (merged from the Party of Patriots of Kazakhstan and the Kazakhstan Social Democratic Party). A court order in August 2015 closed the Communist Party of Kazakhstan for not having the minimum number of members. One party remained registered although it was defunct, leaving six functioning parties. The parties generally did not oppose President Nazarbayev's policies.

In order to register, a political party must hold a founding congress with a minimum attendance of 1,000 delegates, including representatives from two-thirds of the oblasts and the cities of Astana and Almaty. Parties must obtain at least 600 signatures from each oblast and the cities of Astana and Almaty, registration from the Central Election Commission (CEC), and registration from each oblast-level election commission.

Participation of Women and Minorities: Traditional attitudes sometimes hindered women from holding high office or playing active roles in political life, although there were no legal restrictions on the participation of women or minorities in politics.

Section 4. Corruption and Lack of Transparency in Government

The law provides criminal penalties for corruption by officials. The government did not implement the law effectively, and officials frequently engaged in corrupt practices with impunity.

Corruption: Corruption was widespread in the executive branch, law enforcement agencies, local government administrations, the education system, and the judiciary, according to opposition leaders and human rights NGOs. The Ministry of Internal Affairs, the Agency on Civil Service Affairs and Combatting Corruption, the KNB, and the Disciplinary State Service Commission are responsible for combating corruption. According to official statistics, 2,928 corruption-related offenses were registered during the year, and 1,692 cases were submitted to courts.

On June 9, a criminal court in Astana sentenced Talgat Yermegiyayev, the former CEO of Astana Expo 2017, to 14 years in high-security prison for embezzlement. Twenty-three other officials were convicted. Twelve received lesser punishment due to cooperation with the investigation, full admission of guilt, and repayment of damages. The rest were punished by harsher sentences of five to eight years in prison. Yermegiyayev's appeal was denied by the court of appeals on August 9.

The new criminal code toughened criminal liability and punishment for crimes related to corruption. It does not allow probation for corruption crimes. There is also an additional penalty of a lifetime ban on employment in the civil service, as well as mandatory forfeiture of titles, ranks, grades, and state awards. The statute of limitation does not apply to persons charged with corruption.

Financial Disclosure: The law requires government officials, applicants for government positions, and those recently released from government service to declare their income and assets in the country and abroad to tax authorities annually. The same requirement applies to their spouses, dependents, and adult children. Similar regulations exist for members of parliament and judges. Tax declarations are not available to the public. The law imposes administrative penalties for noncompliance with the requirements.

Public Access to Information: Although the law mandates that the government, public associations, officials, and media outlets provide citizens with information that affects their rights and interests, citizen requests for information were not properly fulfilled. NGOs reported problems with access to information from government agencies, citing red tape, poor content on official websites, and poor quality of results.

The Ministry of Information and Communication noted significant progress in providing public access to information and named the Ministry of Healthcare and Social Development as fully complying with the law. Parliamentarians noted problems, however, with access to information from government agencies, poor content on official websites, and poor quality of results.

The law requires government bodies, national companies, quasi-government organizations, and monopolies to provide specified information to the public, along with transparency of any information concerning the government's budget and its expenditures. The law toughens requirements for the composition of information on the websites of the institutions. Additionally, meetings of government bodies, local executive offices, and open meetings of the parliament are required to have live online broadcasting. The law calls for a list to be prepared of information that must be disclosed to the public.

Although parliament published several draft laws, some parliamentary debates, and occasionally its recorded votes, many parliamentary activities took place outside public view. Accredited journalists and representatives of public associations could observe some parliamentary sessions via video link from a separate room. Transcripts of parliamentary sessions were not available to the public. Parliament continued to prohibit public and media access to discussion of controversial legislation.

Section 5. Governmental Attitude Regarding International and Nongovernmental Investigation of Alleged Violations of Human Rights

A number of domestic and international human rights groups operated with some freedom to investigate and publish their findings on human rights cases, although some restrictions on human rights NGO activities remained. International and local human rights groups reported the government monitored NGO activities on sensitive issues and practiced harassment, including police visits to and surveillance of NGO offices, personnel, and family members. Government officials often were uncooperative or nonresponsive to their views.

The Ministry of Foreign Affairs-led Consultative Advisory Body (CAB) for dialogue on democracy, human rights, rule of law, and legislative work continued to operate during the year. The CAB includes government ministries and prominent international and domestic NGOs, as well as international organizations as observers. The NGO community generally was positive about the work of the

CAB, saying the platform enabled greater communication with the government about issues of concern. The government and NGOs, however, did not agree on recommendations on issues the government considered sensitive, and some human rights concerns were barred from discussion. NGOs reported that government bodies accepted some recommendations, although the accepted recommendations were technical rather than substantive.

KIBHR, Adil Soz, Freedom House, and PRI were among the most visibly active human rights NGOs. Some NGOs faced occasional difficulties in acquiring office space and technical facilities. Government leaders participated in--and included NGOs in--roundtables and events on democracy and human rights.

The United Nations or Other International Bodies: The government invited UN special rapporteurs to visit the country and meet with NGOs dealing with human rights. The government generally did not prevent other international NGOs and multilateral institutions dealing with human rights from visiting the country and meeting with local human rights groups and government officials. National security laws prohibit foreigners, international organizations, NGOs, and other nonprofit organizations from engaging in political activities. The government prohibited international organizations from funding unregistered entities.

Government Human Rights Bodies: The Presidential Commission on Human Rights is a consultative and advisory body that includes members of the public appointed by the president. The commission reviews and investigates complaints, issues recommendations, monitors fulfillment of international human rights conventions, and publishes annual human rights reports in close cooperation with several international organizations, such as UNHCR, the OSCE, International Organization for Migration, and UN Children's Fund. The commission does not have legal authority to remedy human rights violations or implement its recommendations in the annual human rights reports.

The presidentially appointed human rights ombudsman is the chair of the Coordinating Council of the National Preventive Mechanism against Torture.

The ombudsman did not have the authority to investigate complaints concerning decisions of the president, heads of government agencies, parliament, cabinet, Constitutional Council, Prosecutor General's Office, CEC, or courts, although he may investigate complaints against individuals. The ombudsman's office has the authority to appeal to the president, cabinet, or parliament to resolve citizens' complaints; cooperate with international human rights organizations and NGOs;

meet with government officials concerning human rights violations; visit certain facilities, such as military units and prisons; and publicize in media the results of investigations. The ombudsman's office also published an annual human rights report. During the year the ombudsman's office occasionally briefed media and issued reports on complaints it had investigated.

Domestic human rights observers indicated that the ombudsman's office and the Human Rights Commission were unable to stop human rights abuses or punish perpetrators. The commission and ombudsman avoided addressing underlying structural problems that led to human rights violations, although they advanced human rights by publicizing statistics and individual cases, and aided citizens with less controversial social problems and issues involving lower-level elements of the bureaucracy.

Section 6. Discrimination, Societal Abuses, and Trafficking in Persons

Women

Rape and Domestic Violence: The law criminalizes rape. The punishment for rape, including spousal rape, ranges from three to 15 years' imprisonment. Under the law a prosecutor may not initiate a rape case absent aggravating circumstances, such as gang rape, unless the victim files a complaint. Once a complaint is filed, the criminal investigation may not be dismissed if the rape victim recants or refuses to cooperate further with the investigation. There were reports of police and judicial reluctance to act on reports of rape, particularly in spousal rape cases.

Legislation identifies various types of domestic violence, such as physical, psychological, sexual, and economic, and outlines the responsibilities of local and national governments and NGOs in providing support to domestic violence victims. The law also outlines mechanisms for the issuance of restraining orders and provides for the 24-hour administrative detention of abusers. The law sets the maximum sentence for spousal assault and battery at 10 years in prison, the same as for any assault. The law also permits prohibiting offenders from living with the victim if the perpetrator has somewhere else to live, allows victims of domestic violence to receive appropriate care regardless of the place of residence, and replaces financial penalties with administrative arrest if paying fines was hurting victims as well as perpetrators.

The government stated that domestic violence is a serious problem. NGOs estimated one in four families suffered some form of domestic violence.

Police intervened in family disputes only when they believed the abuse was life threatening. Every regional administrative police unit has a specialist on gender issues, and these specialists are primarily women. Local community police, however, are generally men, and they are the first responders to calls and the first to work with victims. Police often encouraged the two parties to reconcile. Even when a charge was filed, the victim often withdrew the charge later. NGOs reported women often withdrew their complaints because of economic insecurity.

In the aftermath of the 2014 changes to the law on Prevention of Domestic Violence, the government opened domestic violence shelters in each region that did not already have an established shelter. As a result approximately 3,500 women were referred to crisis centers in 2015 for legal and psychological support. According to the Ministry of Internal Affairs, there are 28 crisis centers. They received 20 percent of their funding from the government and 80 percent through international grants from NGOs.

Other Harmful Traditional Practices: Although prohibited by law, the practice of kidnapping women and girls for forced marriage continued in some remote areas. The law prescribes a prison sentence of eight to 10 years for kidnapping. A person who voluntarily releases an abductee is absolved of criminal responsibility if, in this action, he/she did not commit another offense. Because of this law, a typical bride kidnapper is not necessarily held criminally responsible for the act. Cases were typically not pursued, since families and victims usually did not file complaints or withdrew them and found ways to resolve the problem privately. Law enforcement agencies often advised abductees to sort out their situation themselves. According to civil society organizations, making a complaint to police could be a very bureaucratic process and often subjected families and victims to humiliation. If a complaint is filed, the government is obliged to take action on it but rarely did so. The growing number of news stories and publications about bride kidnapping generated strong public reaction.

Sexual Harassment: Sexual harassment remained a problem. The law prohibits some forms of sexual harassment, but legal and gender experts regarded the legislation as inadequate. There were reports of incidents of harassment, but in no instance was the law used to protect the victim, nor were there reports of any prosecutions. No law protects women from sexual harassment, and only force or taking advantage of a victim's physical helplessness carries criminal liability in terms of sexual assault.

Anna Belousova, a cleaner at a primary school in Kostanay region, was harassed by the school director who tried to force her into a sexual relationship with him. She refused and lost her job. After police dismissed Belousova's complaints, she filed a complaint with the UN Committee on the Elimination of Discrimination against Women, which found that Kazakhstan failed to fulfill its obligations under the UN convention and that it should provide appropriate reparation to her for moral and material damages. On September 29, the Kostanay court of appeals rejected her appeal on restitution of damages.

Reproductive Rights: Couples and individuals have the right to decide the number, spacing, and timing of their children and had the means to do so free from discrimination, coercion, or violence. Women and men received equal treatment for sexually transmitted infections. According to a study published by the UN Fund for Population, in 2014 approximately 50 percent of women used some form of contraception.

According to the UN Population Division, an estimated 53 percent of women used a modern method of contraception during the year. According to the UN Population Fund, in 2015 skilled health personnel attended more than 99 percent of births.

Discrimination: The constitution and law provide for equal rights and freedoms for men and women. The law prohibits discrimination based on gender. According to observers, women in rural areas faced greater discrimination than women in urban areas and suffered from a greater incidence of domestic violence, limited education and employment opportunities, limited access to information, and discrimination in their land and other property rights.

Children

On February 10, the president issued a decree to establish the Office of the Commissioner for Child Rights (Children's Ombudsman) to improve the national system of child rights protection. In March a member of the Mazhilis, Zagipa Baliyeva, was appointed commissioner for child rights.

Birth Registration: Citizenship is derived both by birth within the country's territory and from one's parents. The government registers all births upon receipt of the proper paperwork, which can come from the parents, other interested persons, or the medical facility where the birth occurred.

<u>Child Abuse</u>: School violence was a problem, and experts estimated two out of three schoolchildren suffered or witnessed violence. The majority of crimes remained unreported and thus not included in official statistics. An estimated 17,000-18,000 children suffered from either psychological or physical abuse by their parents.

According to UNICEF, 65 percent of respondents applied psychological pressure and 40 percent used corporal punishment to discipline their children. Sixty-two percent of children were subjected to abuse in families. Abuse was more common in rural areas. Minors age 16 or older have the right to file petitions related to their interests directly with a court. According to official statistics, 156 criminal beatings and intentional infliction of bodily harm to children were registered in 2016. The Children's Rights Protection Committee of the Education and Science Ministry reported that nearly 700 parents were deprived of their parental rights in 2015.

The president of the NGO Union of Crisis Centers stated the number of psychological abuse cases exceeded the number of physical abuse cases. In 2016, the union's hotline received 272,953 calls, including 7,707 reported violation of the rights of children. The union's call center received 325 calls on suicide issues, including 164 from children.

There were reported incidents of child selling. In 2015 Shymkent police arrested two doctors of a perinatal center on suspicion of selling newborn babies. On June 20, the Shymkent interdistrict specialized court convicted the two doctors for selling at least 21 babies. The doctors were sentenced to 10 to 11 years in prison. In July a specialized interdistrict court in Almaty convicted 15 doctors and staff of the Almaty clinical hospital who sold babies to childless couples. Sentences varied from two to nine years in prison, depending on the defendant's role in the crimes.

In November an employee of the Mangistau perinatal hospital was sentenced to eight years in prison for sale of newborn babies. A lawyer who helped to fix the paperwork was sentenced to 7.5 years, and one of the mothers was sentenced to five years of imprisonment.

<u>Early and Forced Marriage</u>: The legal minimum age for marriage is 18, but it may be reduced to 16 in the case of pregnancy or mutual agreement. NGOs noted several cases of marriage under 18, especially in the south. According to the NGO League of Women of Creative Initiative, 2,000-3,000 early and forced marriages occur annually. According to the NGO, there were approximately 2,200 such

marriages in 2014. The majority of these were due to cultural traditions. Many couples first married in mosques and then registered officially when the bride reached the legal age. The government did not take any action to address the issue. In September 2015 the Spiritual Administration of Muslims of Kazakhstan issued an order forbidding mosques to conduct religious marriage rites (nikah) without an official marriage certificate, but the practice continued.

Sexual Exploitation of Children: The law does not specify the minimum age for consensual sex, but it provides for eight to 15 years in prison as punishment for individuals who force boys or girls under age 18 to have sexual intercourse. According to official statistics, there were 364 incidents of forced sexual intercourse with minors, and 158 incidents of corruption and seduction of minors were registered in 2016. The Children's Ombudsman noted that the number of sexual violence incidents reported increased 38.2 percent in the country compared with the previous year.

The law criminalizes the production and distribution of child pornography and provides administrative penalties to cover the sale of pornographic materials to minors. The country retains administrative penalties for child pornography. Perpetrators convicted of sexual offenses against minors receive a lifetime ban on working with children.

Displaced Children: According to the Children's Rights Protection Committee, more than 5,000 street children were referred to temporary housing centers for delinquent minors, and from there, 4,993 were sent back to families, 432 to orphanages, and 79 to foster and adoptive families in 2015.

Institutionalized Children: Under the 2015-20 National Plan for Strengthening Family, Moral, Spiritual, and Ethical Values, the country was working to reduce the number of orphanages and referring children to smaller, family-type orphanages and to foster and patronage families. According to the Children's Rights Protection Committee, approximately 8,000 of the country's 30,000 orphaned children lived in 146 orphanages. The rest of the children were in foster or other home care. Incidents of child abuse in state-run institutions, such as orphanages, boarding schools, and detention facilities for delinquent children, were "not rare," according to government sources. NGOs alleged half the children in orphanages or closed institutions suffered from abuse by teachers or other children.

International Child Abductions: The country is a party to the 1980 Hague Convention on the Civil Aspects of International Child Abduction. See the

Department of State's *Annual Report on International Parental Child Abduction* at travel.state.gov/content/childabduction/en/legal/compliance.html.

Anti-Semitism

Approximately 30,000 to 40,000 Jews lived in the country. Leaders of the Jewish community reported no incidents of anti-Semitism by the government or in society.

Trafficking in Persons

See the Department of State's Trafficking in Persons Report at www.state.gov/j/tip/rls/tiprpt/.

Persons with Disabilities

The Ministry of Healthcare and Social Development was the primary government agency responsible for protecting the rights of persons with disabilities. The law prohibits discrimination against persons with physical, sensory, intellectual, and mental disabilities in employment, education, and access to health care, and in the provision of other government services, but significant discrimination existed in the areas of employment, education, and access to government services.

The law provides for access to information for persons with disabilities. The government produced periodicals, scientific journals, reference literature, and fictional works that were recorded either on disc or in Braille. The law requires one national television channel to broadcast news programs with sign-language interpretation. NGOs stated implementation of the law on disability was lacking, and the Nur Otan Party's Institute of Parliamentary Development concluded that access for persons with disabilities to information and communications was insufficient.

The law requires companies to set aside 3 percent of their jobs for persons with disabilities. International and local observers noted some improvement regarding the rights of persons with disabilities. During the year the government showed commitment to addressing the rights of persons with disabilities, including high-level enforcement of measures to enhance their economic opportunities. Nevertheless, there were reports persons with disabilities faced difficulty integrating into society and finding employment. The vice minister of Healthcare and Social Development identified the two biggest problems facing persons with disabilities as poor infrastructure and lack of access to education. Persons with disabilities had difficulty accessing public transportation. The government has enacted high-level enforcement of measures to enhance economic opportunities for citizens with disabilities, part of the president's Strategy 2050.

Citizens with mental disabilities may be committed to state-run institutions without their consent or judicial review, and the government committed young persons under age 18 with the permission of their families. Institutions were poorly managed, understaffed, and inadequately funded.

There are no regulations regarding the rights of patients in mental hospitals. Human rights observers believed this led to widespread abuse of patients' rights. NGOs reported that patients often experienced poor conditions and a complete lack of privacy. According to an NPM report, most of the hospitals required extensive maintenance. Other problems observed included shortage of personnel, unsatisfactory sanitary-hygienic conditions, poor food supply, overcrowding, and lack of light and air.

Members of the NPM may visit mental hospitals to monitor conditions and signs of possible torture of patients, but any institutions holding children, including orphanages, were not on the list of institutions NPM members may visit.

The government did not legally restrict the right of persons with disabilities to vote and arranged home voting for individuals who could not travel to polling places inaccessible to them.

National/Racial/Ethnic Minorities

Kazakh is the official state language, although Russian has equal status as the language of interethnic communication. The law does not require the ability to speak Kazakh for entry into the civil service and prohibits discrimination based on language. Nonetheless, Kazakh language ability is looked upon favorably, which non-Kazakh speakers protested as language discrimination. The law requires presidential candidates to be fluent in Kazakh.

The creation of Kazakh-language schools and the conversion of some Russian-language schools to Kazakh reduced the number of Russian-only language schools.

Acts of Violence, Discrimination, and Other Abuses Based on Sexual Orientation and Gender Identity

According to the constitution, no one shall be subject to any discrimination for reasons of origin; occupational, social, or property status; sex; race; nationality; language; religion or belief; place of residence; or any other circumstances. The country does not criminalize consensual same-sex sexual activity. During the year a law on "protecting the child," which included a provision that would have prohibited "propaganda of nontraditional sexual relations," was discussed in parliament. The Senate chairman sent the law to the Constitutional Council, which declared it unconstitutional.

Although gender reassignment documentation exists, the law requires a transgender person to fulfill three steps before being able to receive identity documents that align with the person's outward gender: (1) a month of inpatient psychiatric evaluation, (2) a course of hormone replacement therapy, and (3) approval and completion of gender reassignment surgery. Those who receive such surgery outside of the country fall outside this process. Many individuals lived with nonconforming documents for years and reported problems with securing employment, housing, and health care.

According to a 2015 survey, half of transgender persons indicated that they experienced physical abuse due to prejudice against transgender individuals or did not experience such abuse because their gender identity was unknown. NGOs reported court cases on discrimination against sexual minorities.

Although there were no government statistics on discrimination or violence based on sexual orientation or gender identity, there were reports of such actions. According to representatives of international and local organizations, negative social attitudes towards members of marginalized groups, including LGBTI persons, impeded the willingness of the latter to come forward, organize, or seek access to HIV/AIDS programs. Hate crime legislation or other legal mechanisms do not exist to aid prosecution of bias-motivated crimes against members of the LGBTI community. There were no prosecutions of anti-LGBTI violence.

NGOs reported members of the LGBTI community seldom turned to law enforcement agencies to report violence against them because they feared hostility, ridicule, and occasionally violence. They were reluctant to use mechanisms such as the national commissioner for human rights to seek remedies for harms inflicted, because they did not trust these mechanisms to safeguard their identities, especially with regard to employment.

HIV and AIDS Social Stigma

The law prohibits discrimination against persons with HIV and AIDS. Observers reported cultural stigma against drug users and other at-risk groups resulted in societal discrimination that continued to affect access to information, services, treatment, and care. The National Center for AIDS provides free diagnosis and treatment to all citizens. Several NGOs under the Association for Kazakhstan's People Living with AIDS help solve social and economic problems related to diagnosing and living with AIDS. They work with sex workers, the LGBTI community, and injection drug users.

Section 7. Worker Rights

a. Freedom of Association and the Right to Collective Bargaining

The law protects workers' right to unionize but jeopardizes workers' freedom of association.

A trade union law passed and entered into force in 2014 restricts worker freedom of association by requiring existing independent labor unions to affiliate with larger unions at the industry, sector, or regional level and by erecting significant barriers to the creation of new independent unions. The law gave existing unions until mid-2015 to reregister. In June 2015, one month before the reregistration deadline, there were 896 unions in the country. As of the end of September, the country had three re-registered and reorganized national unions. Two independent labor unions, the Confederation of the Independent Trade Unions of Kazakhstan (CITUK) and the Kazakhstan's Confederation of Labor, were reregistered after months of bureaucratic delays, though a court case was initiated by the Ministry of Justice against CITUK in December to close the trade union for insufficient regional registration. The third reregistered national union, the Federation of Trade Unions of the Republic of Kazakhstan (FPRK), is the successor to state-sponsored Soviet-era labor organizations and the largest national trade union association, with approximately 90 percent of union workers on its rolls. The government exercised considerable influence on organized labor and favored state-affiliated unions over independent ones. Critics charged that the federation was too close to the government to advocate for workers effectively and that the new law helped the federation in its unfair competition against independent labor unions. The 2014 law requires labor unions that are independent to affiliate with larger, progovernment ones, violating the country's obligations under international labor standards on freedom of association. Labor officials argued that requiring smaller and independent unions to affiliate with larger ones would make them more effective and improve their ability to bargain collectively, thus preventing labor disputes and social unrest. As of January one-third of the country's working population was unionized.

Early in the year, one labor rights activist filed a suit against parliament, claiming that some provisions of the labor union law were unconstitutional. The court declined the claim on the plea of noncompliance with internal procedures of lawsuit filing. As a result, the hearings did not happen.

The law protects the right of workers to bargain collectively. It provides that an individual contract between an employer and an employee sets the employee's wage and outlines the rights and responsibilities of the employee and the employer. The law protects workers against antiunion discrimination, and a court may order reinstatement of a worker fired for union activity. According to the FPRK data, 97 percent of unionized enterprises have collective agreements.

The law protects the right to strike in principle but imposes onerous restrictions that make strikes less effective, impose severe penalties, or deny the right to strike to a variety of workers.

A blanket legal restriction bars certain occupations from striking. Military and other security service members, emergency medical, fire, and rescue crews, as well as those who operate "dangerous" production facilities are forbidden to strike. Under the law such strikes are illegal.

Workers employed in the railway, transport and communications, civil aviation, health-care, and public utilities sectors may strike, but only if they maintain minimum services, do not interrupt nonstop production processes (such as metallurgy), and leave key equipment unaffected.

Numerous legal limitations restrict workers' right to strike in other industries as well. Generally, workers may not strike unless a labor dispute cannot be resolved through compulsory arbitration procedures. Decisions to strike must be taken in a meeting where at least one-half of an enterprise's workers are present. A written notice announcing a strike must be submitted to the employer at least five days in advance. Employers may fire striking workers after a court declares a strike illegal. The law enables the government to target labor organizers whose strikes are deemed illegal. The legal changes set stiff penalties for those who participate in strikes deemed illegal, a point that aroused special concern because judges responsible for determining whether a strike is illegal lacked independence. Thus, observers were concerned the provisions were more likely to be used to target labor organizers unfairly.

A new labor code, signed into law in November 2015, also limits worker rights to make claims on their employers. For example, its Article 11 requires employers to negotiate any labor-related act with official employee representatives. If there are multiple official representatives, they have three days in which to form a unified body to discuss the proposed act. If the group cannot come to consensus, any one representative may accept the act without the consent of the others. Article 49 includes 27 new reasons an employer may fire a worker.

Disagreements between unions and their employers may be presented to a tripartite commission composed of representatives of the government, labor unions, and employer associations. State-affiliated and independent labor unions participate in tripartite commissions. The tripartite commission is responsible for developing and signing annual agreements governing most aspects of labor relations.

Foreign workers have the right to join unions, but the law prohibits the operation of foreign unions and the financing of unions by foreign entities, such as foreign citizens, governments, and international organizations. Irregular migrants and self-employed individuals resided in the country and were not per se exempt from the law. Approximately 2.3 million of the nine million economically active citizens were self-employed in 2015.

b. Prohibition of Forced or Compulsory Labor

The law prohibits all forms of forced or compulsory labor, except when it is a consequence of a court sentencing or a condition of a state of emergency or martial law.

Violations of labor law may result in an administrative penalty, such as a fine, or in civil or criminal liability. Penalties were generally sufficient to deter violations, and recent amendments significantly increased criminal punishment for some labor crimes against minors. The Ministry of Healthcare and Social Development is responsible for conducting checks of employers to reveal labor violations, including foreign labor. In 2015, however, its functions were transferred to local government. The Law on State Control of 2011 codifies the right of labor inspectors to conduct announced and unannounced inspections of workplaces to detect safety and other violations, but on January 1, that law was superseded by the Entrepreneur Code (adopted in October 2015). In 2015 labor inspectors did not conduct inspections due to a moratorium on inspections of small- and medium-size businesses introduced by the president's Decree No. 757, issued in 2014 as part of an effort to address petty corruption, which prohibited announced inspections as of January 1, 2015. Labor inspectors may only conduct unannounced inspections of businesses if they have evidence of labor violations. During the year labor inspections were renewed; however, no statistics were available on the number of violations revealed during the checks. The Ministry of Internal Affairs is also responsible for identifying victims of forced labor and initiating criminal proceedings. Police conducted interagency operations to find victims of forced labor and trafficking.

Forced labor occurred. Migrant workers were considered most at risk for forced or compulsory labor. Reports varied on the number of labor migrants in the country. Estimates ranged from 300,000 to 750,000, with the majority of migrant workers coming from Uzbekistan, Tajikistan, and Kyrgyzstan. Migrant workers found employment primarily in agriculture and construction. The Ministry of Healthcare and Social Development is responsible for handling issues related to migrant labor.

Also see the Department of State's *Trafficking in Persons Report* at www.state.gov/j/tip/rls/tiprpt/.

c. Prohibition of Child Labor and Minimum Age for Employment

The general minimum age for employment is 16. With parental permission, however, children ages 14-16 may perform light work that does not interfere with their health or education. The law also restricts the length of the workday for employees younger than 18.

The Ministry of Healthcare and Social Development is responsible for enforcement of child labor laws and for administrative offenses punishable by fines. Noncriminal punishments include written warnings, suspensions, terminations, the withdrawal of licenses for specific types of activities, administrative penalties or fines, and administrative arrests (only by court decision and up to 15 days) for violations of legislation including in relation to minors. Under the new administrative code, employment of a minor without an employment agreement is punishable by up to 200 monthly calculation index (MCI) units ($1,250) with suspension of the employer's license. Untimely or incorrectly paid salaries are also punishable by fines of up to 150 MCI ($935); nonprovision of vacations, up to 100 MCI ($624); illegal excessive work hours, up to 120 MCI ($748); and discrimination at the workplace, up to 200 MCI ($1,250).

In January 2015 new amendments to penal and administrative codes came into force that strengthen criminal punishment for labor and sex exploitation crimes committed against minors. For example, a lifetime ban of activities or work with children is introduced for those who have committed crimes such as coercion of minors into illegal activities, including begging, coercion of minors into prostitution, production and distribution of materials or objects that contain pornographic images of minors, or engaging minors in pornographic shows. Punishment for the last crime also increased from eight to 10 years in prison. The fines for violation of labor legislation in relation to minors (Article 153), including violation of minimum age for employment in hazardous work, increased nearly sevenfold under the new penal code from 300 MCI units to 2,000 MCI units. The same crime committed by a group of persons, repeatedly, in relation to two or more minors, in relation to a minor known to be suffering from a mental disorder or in a helpless condition, or by a person in a position of trust (such as a parent or teacher) is punishable by a fine in an amount up to 5,000 MCI units or imprisonment up to five years.

The Ministry of Internal Affairs is responsible for investigating criminal offenses and trains criminal and migration police in investigating the worst forms of child labor. NGOs reported some instances of child labor in domestic servitude, markets, construction sites, and activities such as car washes, cultivation of vegetables, and begging. Media reported instances of child labor in cotton farming in Maktaralskyi District of South Kazakhstan. The government cooperated with trade unions, employers, and NGOs to raise awareness of and promote interagency cooperation in eliminating child labor.

Also see the Department of Labor's *Findings on the Worst Forms of Child Labor* at www.dol.gov/ilab/reports/child-labor/findings/.

d. Discrimination with Respect to Employment and Occupation

Law and regulations prohibit discrimination with respect to employment and occupation based on gender, age, disability, race, ethnicity, language, place of residence, religion, political opinion, affiliation with tribe or class, public associations, or property, social, or official status. The law does not specifically prohibit discrimination with respect to employment and occupation based on disability, sexual orientation, gender identity, age, HIV-positive status, or having other communicable diseases. The government effectively enforced the law and regulations. Discrimination is a criminal offense punishable by a fine up to

991,000 tenge ($2,970) or imprisonment for up to 90 days, which was generally sufficient to deter violations.

Discrimination, however, occurred with respect to employment and occupation for persons with disabilities, orphans, and former convicts. Disability NGOs reported that despite government efforts, obtaining employment was difficult. The law does not require equal pay for equal work for women and men. NGOs reported no government body assumed responsibility for implementing antidiscrimination legislation and asserted the law's definition of gender discrimination does not comply with international standards. More women than men were self-employed or underemployed relative to their education level.

e. Acceptable Conditions of Work

During the year the national monthly minimum wage was 22,859 tenge ($67). Most workers earned above the minimum wage in urban areas. In 2015, 2.7 percent of the population lived below the monthly subsistence income level of 19,647 tenge ($59). In 2015, 23 percent of the working population worked in the informal economy.

The law stipulates the normal workweek should not exceed 40 hours and limits heavy manual labor or hazardous work to no more than 36 hours per week. The law limits overtime to two hours per day, or one hour per day for heavy manual labor, and requires overtime to be paid at least at a 50-percent premium. The law prohibits compulsory overtime and overtime for work in hazardous conditions. The law provides that labor agreements may stipulate the length of working time, holidays, and paid annual leave for each worker. The government sets occupational health and safety standards. The law requires employers to suspend work that could endanger the life or health of workers and to warn workers about any harmful or dangerous work conditions or the possibility of any occupational disease. The law specifically grants workers the right to remove themselves from situations that endanger their health or safety without suffering adverse employment action.

The new labor code reduced overtime pay for holiday and after-hours work to 1.25 times regular salary, compared with previous rates of 2 and 1.5 times, respectively. The new code also removed provisions requiring a minimum wage for work in hazardous conditions. Under the previous law, a tripartite commission was charged with negotiating and determining a minimum wage for miners, metallurgists, and others working in hazardous industries.

The Ministry of Healthcare and Social Development enforces the minimum wage, work-hour restrictions, overtime, and occupational safety and health standards. The law codifies the right of government labor inspectors to conduct unannounced inspections of workplaces to detect safety and other violations. Ministry inspectors conducted random inspections of employers. The ministry had 258 labor inspectors. The Human Rights Commission reported that the number of inspectors was insufficient. Moreover, a new labor code introduced so-called employer's declarations. Under the new system, labor inspectors may extend a certificate of trust to enterprises that complied with labor legislation requirements. Certified enterprises are exempt from labor inspections for the three-year period. In the opinion of labor rights activists, such a practice may worsen labor conditions and conceal problems. The new labor code introduced a new body for addressing labor safety issues, to be called a production council. Any enterprise or company may form such a council that would be composed of representatives of an employer and employees. Councils are eligible to conduct their own inspections of the employees' work conditions.

There were reports some employers ignored regulations concerning occupational health and safety. Occupational safety and health conditions in the construction, industrial, and agricultural sectors often were substandard. Workers in factories sometimes lacked quality protective clothing and sometimes worked in conditions of poor visibility and ventilation. Some companies are trying to avoid payments to injured workers. A copper giant, KazakhMys, established a special division, the main goal of which is to investigate every case of industrial injury. A minimal noncompliance with labor safety requirements may result in a company's refusal to pay workers industrial injury compensations.

In the first half of the year, the government reported 840 individuals injured at their workplaces and 112 workplace deaths. The government attributed many labor-related deaths to antiquated equipment, insufficient detection and prevention of occupational diseases in workers engaged in harmful labor, and disregard for safety regulations. The most dangerous jobs were in mining, construction, and oil and gas, according to an expert analysis of occupations with the highest fatalities.

In 2015 workers in the informal economy made up 23 percent of the working population. The informal economy is mostly concentrated in the retail trade, transport services, agriculture, real estate, beauty and hair dressing salons, and laundry and dry cleaning businesses. Small entrepreneurs and their employees for the most part work without health, social, or pension benefits.

www.ingramcontent.com/pod-product-compliance
Lightning Source LLC
Chambersburg PA
CBHW080816280726
48660CB00018B/3481